I Can

Write an Extraordinary College Essay

by Ashley Schmitt
www.CollegeEssayNinja.com

Table of Contents

Chapter 1

What Will I Get Out of this Book?

You may be asking yourself "Why should I read this book?" "What will I get out of it?" This book was designed with you, a high school student, in mind. The writing is straight forward, easy to read, without filler or fluff, and packed with lots of examples that are based on real students' experiences. The methods taught in this book are simple to understand and are very effective when applied. The methods taught are similar and complimentary to my other book I Can Ace My College Interview. I recommend picking it up if you need to accomplish any college interviews. While the approach to both essay and interview questions are similar, this book focuses on the nuisances of an essay.

I based this book on my experience working as a Regional Director of Admissions at a prestigious university and working with students to help brainstorm and prepare college essays. I sat on Admissions Panels and have reviewed thousands upon thousands of student files for admissions. I hate to say it, but many of the applications began to look very much alike. Amazing students, like yourself, become no more than a name in a file. After reading thousands of files you start to see what type of answers set students' essays apart. The student that writes essays like a master storyteller are the ones that connect with the Admissions Officers. Their unique "voice" stands out and Admissions Officers take notice. The simple stories about a student's life resonate with those reading the essay.

"What? I have to be a master storyteller?"

Yes, you do. But do not fret it is a skill that can be learned. This book will teach you how to become a master storyteller in a simple step-by-step method. It offers topics to avoid, goes through the most common questions, gives strategies to brainstorm ideas, offers example answers, gives strategies to review and edit essays, and has checklists for after you have written your essays. You CAN write an extraordinary college essay that is interesting and will make Admissions Officers take notice.

I want to emphasize that being interesting and fascinating does not mean that you must have traveled the world, baked a two-story tall cupcake, been on television, or anything crazy. People are ALL fascinating; it is the little details about our lives that make us unique and interesting to others. I will say that again it is the *little details* that make us unique. In broad sweeps many of us sound or appear alike. For example, you can group students by SAT/ACTs and grades. Those within certain ranges have very similar profiles, similar scores, similar grades, and many times the same activities. That is what Admissions Officers see. They see a set of students within a certain range. The broad stroke approach makes all the students look the same. As an Admissions Officer, I knew they were not the same. I tried to dig a little deeper and look for interesting details that made the person unique.

I found that many students only gave vague details with no interest or color. I pulled out very little that seemed different. Some students were the exception. They gave me colorful stories and insight into how and why they thought a certain way. These students stood out to me. The students, whose files I carefully read and made sure to consider for admission. The details matter. They can make a difference.

The stories about you and your life matter. They make you the unique person you are. This book was written to help you search inside yourself for the details. To find the interesting, daily events that are golden nuggets and make excellent essays. This book will help you craft those stories into amazing essays about your life. Essays that make Admissions Officers remember you and seriously consider you as a candidate for your chosen university.

Good Luck and for more information or books about college essays or interviews check us out at
www.CollegeEssayNinja.com

Chapter 2

Think Like an Admissions Officer

The purpose of written essays is to see a side of you that is not reflected through your grades or activities. A person cannot be reduced to a transcript, SAT/ACT scores, or a resume. People are far more interesting and complex than that. The essay questions are a chance for the Admissions Officer to see beyond your academic scores and beyond your list of activities. Done correctly, your essays should transform you from a file into a real live person. To get into your choice school you NEED to become a three-dimensional person with interesting stories and human depth. The essays are your chance to do this!

Now, try to think like an Admissions Officer. They must pick from a list of students who should attend the college. They have a bunch of files with resumes, essays and transcripts. Everybody has a good GPA. Everyone has good SAT scores and ACT scores. Everyone has a huge list of activities. Over half are Captain of some sports team. The other half are on the short list for valedictorian. Some are sports team Captains and valedictorians. The competition is fierce.

Unfortunately, this mass group of students with grades, test scores, and various honors look very similar. If you do not take care with your essays, you will look like everyone else on paper. But you are NOT like everyone else. You are unique, interesting, and most of all you REALLY want to go to the university or college of your choice. So, how can you stand out? You need to make sure your essays reflect you and your personality. You need to make sure that when the Admissions Officer reads your essay they "see" you. Seeing means depicting a picture or a scene. Seeing means stories that evoke a clear view of what is happening or emotion. We'll go over this more later, but for now, know that you need to tell a story that will allow someone to "see" who you are through your actions during the story.

Whenever you turn something in for a grade or for any sort of evaluation you need to think like the person reviewing it. In this case, it is an essay for a College Admissions Officer. Admissions Officers are interested in filling the college or university with the best students possible. Now, best does not always mean the best grades. Best includes a wide variety of students that will make the campus a better place. You may not be the best student in Math, but maybe you are an excellent leader who will be able to organize volunteer groups that help boost the college's standing in the community. Best is very subjective. Before you sell yourself short, think about ways you can help any college campus with your unique talents. I promise that Admissions Officers ARE looking for unique talents that can benefit the college.

In general, most universities and colleges are interested in seeing that a student has acceptable/good grades and participates in a variety of activities. They are looking for examples of leadership, character, an interest in helping others, and being able to think through problems. They want to see that you participate in more than just academics. They are interested in seeing student who take part in various activities like sports, music, clubs, and community involvement.

I tend to generalize what Admissions Officers are looking for into the categories below.

Leadership: An Admissions Officer wants to see examples that depict your problem solving skills, ability to take and give direction, and ability to work with a variety of people. They want someone with vision who can help and serve others in the campus community.

Character: An Admissions Officer wants to see examples of integrity. Examples that show you have solid integrity under pressure. (This is especially true for colleges who pride themselves on their honor code.)

Participation in a variety of activities: An Admissions Officer wants to see examples that you participate in a variety of school activities like sports, clubs, choir, band, and school leadership. An Admissions Officer wants examples of community involvement, such as church, volunteer work, community activities, recreational sports, and work experience. College is more than an academic experience it is a complete learning experience to include all the social and interaction experiences. An Admissions Officer wants to see that you will enhance the campus with your unique talents and work with others around you to the benefit of all. An Admissions Officer does not expect that you have participated in all the listed activities. Instead they are looking to see you have participated in a variety of things from each of these categories. Variety is the key word. Not just sports, not just school clubs, and not just volunteer work.

True interest in the university: The Admissions Officer wants to see examples that you have a real interest in university. You need to know something about the university and why you want to go there.

Did you notice anything similar across those categories? EXAMPLES. Yes they want to see examples, but not just any example. Remember think like an Admissions Officer. They have your resume, scores, and transcript. Your essay must reflect something new about you; something not in your resume or transcript. Otherwise you have missed a golden opportunity. Your essay examples need to be narrative stories or antidotes about you and your involvement in leadership, character, activities, and knowledge about the college.

They want to know about you. They want to know details that make you different from everyone else. Example stories give you life and give you a third dimension that other students will not have. An Admissions Officer wants to be able to decide if you are someone who will be able to handle the challenging social and academic environment of the college. College is sometimes stressful and academically demanding. They need to know whomever they pick will be able to handle those stresses, succeed and make the campus a more interesting/better place. They are trying to determine if you will be able to organize your time and juggle multiple activities. You need to think from that point of view as you create your examples. An Admissions Officer will determine what type of person you are based on your past performance. The better and more detailed your stories, the better they can predict your future success.

To do this you need to brag about yourself through your example stories. But flat out bragging can come across as rude and hard to read about. You probably know someone that you hate to be around because all they do is talk about how wonderful they are. There is a fine line between bragging and showcasing you have what it takes to succeed. Here is the essence of annoying bragging, "I can do this and this and this....." No examples and no engaging story. But there is an acceptable way to brag. The method is called STAR stories. A STAR story offers a way to brag about yourself that sounds very acceptable to people because it comes across as interesting and engages people through the story. Very succinctly, you tell people what you have accomplished in your life and offer results from your actions. An Admissions Officer can then judge for themselves, from your actions and results, if what you accomplished was amazing or not. The STAR story method helps you tell them about yourself in a manner that comes across as very factual and very interesting. You are not bragging. You are showing them about yourself through examples and it really excites an Admissions Officer to hear about students doing amazing things.

Chapter 3

Topics to Avoid

Please, please, please avoid all of the following topics for your essays. I have read thousands upon thousands of essays and I can honestly say that the following topics are overdone, not interesting, or not written in an interesting/appropriate manner. There are exceptions to any rule, but I would caution you to avoid these topics. I'll say it again; find something else to write about. I promise you that you have many other life events that you can write about.

Topics to Avoid

A List: If you list anything in an essay you are missing the point completely. Your resume was your list.

Slang: Do not use slang words or texting abbreviations. This is an essay to get into a college or university and proper use of the English language is expected. Another reason is the slang terms may not be understood by the reader. Admissions Officers are not college or high school students so they may not understand what you are trying to say.

Trendy or Pop Culture References: Avoid using these type of references. They might not make sense or have the impact you are looking for.

Sad topics like divorce, death, or loss: I know this is a favorite, but avoid these topics. Death, divorce, and loss are very hard to write about in a manner that comes across as interesting or unique. The stories tend to be depressing and not very unique. You might have an excellent story about loss that you can turn into an uplifting and brilliant essay where you came out a better person. If so try it, but my advice is to avoid these topics.

"The most important thing": The most important thing in my life is…. This is a very boring topic to read about, because it is too general. Also, it can come across to the reader as bragging or self-important.

Sports: Please do not tell the Admissions Officer about a sports injury you overcame or ignored, so you could win the championship, game, or event. This is the most common topic when a student is asked about overcoming a challenge or obstacle. Do not be like everyone else.

"I am so thankful for": Too broad of a topic and usually sounds like bragging or entitled.

Comparisons: Do not compare yourself to other students. Tell the story, tell the facts, and offer your insights and opinions, but stop if you find yourself saying something like, "While my classmates were doing X, I was...." Cut out statements that compare yourself to others and focus on your side of the story. These type of comparisons usually come across as self-important.

Broad volunteer activities to include, Eagle Scouts, Mission Trips or Camps: I am sure these activities sound like great topics, but there are three problems. 1) Everyone writes about them. 2) The topic is too broad and is boring to read about. 3) Everyone talks about them. Do not fear. Your hard work volunteering will not go unacknowledged. You should not talk about these activities in general, but you CAN talk about specific events that occurred during these types of activities. More about that later, but for now do not plan on writing about your trip to Mexico to rebuild a school.

Trips to visit campus: Boring, too broad of a topic, and too many people write about it.

Any event the college sponsored: Same reason as above. Boring, too broad of a topic, and too many people write about it.

Rude or unprofessionally expressed opinions: Your essay is not the time you want to express your opinions in a rude or unprofessional manner. Yes, college is a time to express yourself and learn new things, but you want to get in first. Being rude or unprofessional is a huge turn off for Admissions Officers. You can write about a controversial topic, but keep it professional and factual. Keep offensive opinions and comments to yourself.

Sensitive Topics: Sensitive topics can work, but it is hard to write about them in a way that comes across as interesting. Sensitive topics make people uncomfortable. You want the Admissions Officer to remember you, not try to avoid your file because it upsets them.

Illegal Activities: Avoid these topics. Remember, you want to get in. Writing an essay exposing your less than desirable activities to the college of your choice, will not help you get in. It exposes you to scrutiny you do not want. There are so many other positive things to write about. There is an exception. Some schools might ask you to explain an arrest or expulsion from school, if that applies to you. If so, keep to the facts. Do not blame anyone or offer your opinion on how unfair the teacher was. State circumstance, facts, and most importantly what you learned.

One student made the mistake of bringing a water gun to school and got expelled. He wrote about how he had brought it to school in his car and planned on squirting a friend. A teacher saw it. He was expelled. He had forgotten about the school's policy and admitted to his mistake. He learned to take responsibility for his actions, even if he had intended no harm and forgotten about the rule. He volunteered to brief the school about his mistake so that other students would be aware of the rule and its consequences.

Stick to the facts and keep opinions to yourself. Put the best positive spin on the situation by expressing what you learned.

Remember to Avoid

- Any kind of list
- Slang
- Trendy or Pop Culture References
- Sad topics like divorce, death, or loss
- "The most important thing"
- Sports
- "I am so thankful for"
- Comparisons
- Broad volunteer activities to include
  - Eagle Scouts
  - Mission trips
  - Camps
- Trips to visit the campus
- Any event the college sponsored
- Rude or unprofessionally expressed opinions
- Sensitive topics
- Illegal activities

Chapter 4

Your Key to Success

The way to dazzle an Admissions Officer with your essay is to be a master storyteller. How? Simple, by learning a simple, yet very effective method to address essay questions. This method works for most essay question prompts. Some prompts will not fit this method exactly, but you can adjust or change it slightly to work with any question. Your key to successfully writing an extraordinary essay is using the STAR story technique. STAR stands for:

STAR
S: Situation
T: Task
A: Action
R: Result or Results

This method is an extremely effective way to frame the experiences in your life and become a master storyteller. Each part of the STAR acronym is important, but the last two (your actions, your results) are probably the most important and where you should spend the most time explaining. I want to highlight one other item. This is a STAR story not a STAR list. You want to create a story and something memorable. Most students and actually most adults when asked any question about themselves start to list a bunch of qualities or offer a vague description. This is not very interesting and does not tell an Admissions Officer anything new. You need to compose stories that display the unique, specific events in your life that shape who you are.

Let's break down the STAR acronym further and look a little deeper into each letter.

STAR
S: Situation; Start with the Problem; Make us "see/feel" it
T: Task; What do you have to do or what problem do you have to solve?
A: Action; What SPECIFICALLY did you do?
R: Results; Lessons learned; How can it apply to you, your life, your world view?

So, how do you create a STAR story? Take events in your life where you have accomplished something, lead an activity, helped someone, saw someone compromising their integrity, got through a difficult time in your life, solved a challenging problem, or confronted a teacher or coach on an issue that meant a lot to you. Got an event in mind? Start with the S, write down a few thoughts and repeat for each letter of STAR.

Did you outline something? Don't worry there are two brainstorming exercises next to help you come up with ideas. In the next chapter, there is a discussion on specific application methods with example essay prompts and an example answer. You will get lots of practice.

Brainstorming STAR stories

I have an activity for you to complete at the end of this section that will help brainstorm STAR stories. With it I want you to come up with eight or nine ideas for STAR stories. If you can come up with more, great! But at least eight or nine. You will use the generated ideas in Chapter 5: How to Tackle Common Questions (with Examples).

You need to vary the examples throughout your life. Do not pull every example from sports. Do not pull every example from academics. Provide examples from several of your activities. For example, one about academics, one about sports, one about leadership in your church, one about school involvement, one about a community activity, and one about a club. Pick examples from all over your life.

Brainstorming Activity #1

IMPORTANT: The purpose of this activity is to get you thinking. Look at each word and ask yourself if you can think of ANY examples, unique stories, or thoughts you can associate with that word. If you think of something, jot a note down or circle the word. As you go through the list you will notice that certain activities or stories will come up several times. Those ones are most likely good STAR stories. Write the ideas and thoughts down for later use. You can use the ideas generated for the Chapter 5: How to Tackle Common Questions (with Examples). If you come up with extra that is great, but make sure to come up with eight or nine in total.

LIST

Adapted (teaching styles/special tools)
Administered (programs)
Advised (people/peers/job-seekers)
Analyzed (data/blueprints/schematics/policies)
Appraised (services/value)
Arranged (meetings/events/training programs)
Assembled (automobiles/computers/apparatus)
Audited (financial records/accounts payable)
Budgeted (expenses)
Calculated (numerical data/annual costs/mileage)
Cataloged (art collection/technical publications)
Checked (accuracy/other's work)
Classified (documents/plants/animals)
Cleaned (houses/auto parts)
Coached (teams/students/athletes)
Collected (money/survey information/data/samples)
Compiled (statistics/survey data)
Confronted (people/difficult issues)
Constructed (buildings)
Consulted (on new designs/investment strategy)
Coordinated (events/work schedules)
Corresponded (with other departments/colleagues)
Counseled (students/peers/job-seekers)
Created (new programs/artwork/internet sites)
Cut (diamonds/concrete/fabric/glass/lumber)

Decided (which equipment to buy/priorities)
Delegated (authority)
Designed (data systems/greeting cards)
Directed (administrative staff/theatre productions)
Dispensed (medication/information)
Displayed (results/products/artifacts)
Distributed (products/mail)
Dramatized (ideas/problems/plays)
Edited (publications/video tape/)
Entertained (people)
Established (objectives/guidelines/policies)
Estimated (physical space/costs/staffing needs)
Evaluated (programs/instructors/peers/students)
Exhibited (plans/public displays/evidence)
Expressed (interest in development projects)
Facilitated (multimedia exhibit/conflict resolution)
Found (missing persons/appropriate housing)
Framed (houses/pictures)
Generated (interest/support)
Grew (plants/vegetables/flowers)
Handled (detailed work/data/complaints/toxins)
Hosted (panel discussions/foreign students)
Implemented (registration system/new programs)
Improved (maintenance schedule/systems)
Initiated (production/changes/improvements)
Inspected (physical objects/repairs/electrical work)
Installed (software/bathrooms/electrical systems/parts)
Interpreted (languages/new laws/schematics/codes)
Interviewed (people/new employees)
Invented (new ideas/machine parts)
Investigated (problems/violations/fraud)
Landscaped (gardens/public parks/indoor gardens)
Led (foreign tours/campus tours)
Listened (to others/to conference calls)
Located (missing information/facilities)
Maintained (transportation fleet/aircraft/diesel engines)
Managed (an organization/a mail room/a retail store)
Measured (boundaries/property lines/bridge clearance)
Mediated (between people/civil settlements)

Met (with dignitaries/public/community groups)
Monitored (progress of others/water flow/electric usage)
Motivated (workers/trainees)
Negotiated (contracts/sales/labor disputes)
Operated (equipment/hydraulic test stand/robotics equipment)
Organized (tasks/library books/data bases)
Painted (houses/cars/aircraft/interiors)
Patrolled (runways/public places/property/buildings)
Persuaded (others/customers)
Planned (agendas/international conferences)
Predicted (future needs/stock market trends)
Presented (major selling points/new products)
Prepared (reports/meals/presentations)
Printed (books/reports/posters)
Processed (human interactions)
Programmed (computers)
Promoted (events/new products/new technology)
Proofread (news/reports/training materials)
Protected (property/people)
Published (reports/books/software)
Purchased (equipment/supplies/services)
Questioned (people/survey participants/suspects/witnesses)
Raised (performance standards/capital investments)
Read (volumes of material/news releases)
Recorded (data/sales totals/music/video)
Recruited (people for hire/executives/Marines)
Rehabilitated (people/old buildings)
Repaired (mechanical devices/exhaust systems)
Reported (findings/monthly activity)
Researched (library documents/cancer/diseases)
Renewed (programs/contracts/insurance policies)
Reviewed (program objectives/books and movies)
Revised (instructional materials)
Scheduled (social events/doctor's appointments)
Sold (advertising space/real estate/cars)
Served (individuals)
Sewed (parachutes/clothing/upholstery)
Signed (for the hearing impaired)
Sketched (charts and diagrams)

Spoke (in public)
Supervised (others)
Taught (classes/math/science)
Tailored (clothing/services)
Televised (conferences/training/events/shows)
Tested (new designs/students/employees)
Updated (files)
Verified (reports/identity)
Volunteered (services/time)
Wrote (reports/training manuals)
Weighed (trucks/patients/precious metals)
Welded (bike frames/airframes/alloys)
X-rayed (limbs/stressed equipment)

Brainstorming Activity #2

How did you do on Brainstorming Activity #1? Did you get eight or nine ideas? If not, that's okay. Brainstorming Activity #2 will hopefully generate a few more ideas.

Activity #2 looks at your defining qualities. A defining quality is a characteristic or personality trait that describes you. It would answer questions such as: What are your best characteristics? How would a friend or family member describe you? What are your strengths? Look through the list below. Circle or jot down about ten characteristics that define you. Try to include a few characteristics that would be beneficial to the major or subjects you are interested in studying. For example if you want to be an engineer; logical, problem-solver, or creative might be good choices. This list is not all inclusive. It is to help you generate ideas. If you come up with a characteristic not listed make sure to look for the positive version of the characteristic. For example, stubborn, a positive spin on this is determined.

Able
Active
Adaptable
Admirable
Adventurous
Agreeable
Alert
Ambitious
Amiable
Amusing
Anticipative
Appreciative
Artful
Articulate
Aspiring
Athletic
Attractive
Balanced
Benevolent
Big-thinking
Bold
Brave
Brilliant
Businesslike
Busy
Calm
Capable
Captivating
Caring
Casual
Challenging

Charismatic
Charitable
Charming
Cheerful
Clean
Clear-headed
Clever
Colorful
Compassionate
Competitive
Complex
Conciliatory
Confident
Confidential
Conscientious
Conservative
Considerate
Constant
Contemplative
Cooperative
Courageous
Courteous
Creative
Cultured
Curious
Daring
Debonair
Decisive
Dedicated
Deep
Determined

Dignified

Direct

Disciplined

Discreet

Dramatic

Dutiful

Dynamic

Eager

Earnest

Efficient

Elegant

Empathetic

Energetic

Enthusiastic

Exciting

Extraordinary

Fair

Faithful

Farsighted

Fast-Learner

Firm

Flexible

Focused

Forceful

Forgiving

Formal

Forthright

Freethinking

Freewheeling

Friendly

Frugal

Fun-loving

Gallant

Generous

Gentle

Genuine

Good-natured

Gracious

Hardworking

Hearty

Helpful

Heroic

High-spirited

Honest

Honorable

Humble

Humorous

Idealistic

Imaginative

Impressive

Independent

Individualistic

Innovative

Inoffensive

Insightful

Inspirational

Intelligent

Intense

Intuitive

Invulnerable

Kind

Knowledgeable

Leader

Liberal

Logical

Lovable

Loyal

Lyrical

Magnanimous

Meticulous

Mature

Methodical

Moderate

Modest

Multi-leveled

Neat

Objective

Observant

Open
Optimistic
Orderly
Organized
Original
Painstaking
Passionate
Patient
Patriotic
Peaceful
Perceptive
Perfectionist
Personable
Persuasive
Planner
Playful
Polished
Popular
Practical
Precise
Principled
Problem-Solver
Profound
Protective
Prudent
Purposeful
Punctual
Questioning
Quiet
Rational
Realistic
Reflective
Relaxed
Reliable
Resourceful
Respectful
Responsible
Responsive
Reverential

Romantic
Rustic
Sage
Scholarly
Scrupulous
Secure
Selfless
Self-reliant
Self-sufficient
Sensitive
Sentimental
Serious
Sharing
Shrewd
Simple
Sincere
Skillful
Sociable
Solid
Sophisticated
Spontaneous
Steadfast
Steady
Stoic
Strong
Studious
Suave
Subtle
Successful
Sympathetic
Systematic
Tasteful
Thorough
Tidy
Tolerant
Tractable
Uncomplaining
Understanding
Unique

Venturesome	Whimsical
Vivacious	Winning
Warm	Wise
Well-rounded	Witty

Now you have completed the two Brainstorming Activities look at your list of activities and characteristics. Do you see any activities, events, stories that line up with your characteristics? If you do, make sure to write down the connections as soon as you see them.

VERY IMPORTANT: I want to mention this point right now as you review your two lists. The stories you are looking for and want to write about in your essay are specific, small moments in your life. Most likely you will overlook these moments, if I didn't force this issue now. There is something about the college application that makes students feel they have to write about some amazing grand event. Not true, for a few reasons.

1) Essays are meant to be short 500-650 words. You cannot write enough detail about a grand event to make it interesting to the reader. Small moments in time are much better for this length of essay.

2) Grand moments sound much like other students' grand moments. These huge events tend to blur in the mind of an Admissions Officer after reading your 100th essay for the day. Specific events with interesting details are much more

interesting and easier to write about. If I asked you to write about the past month, you would have to think about it, generalize what you did, and maybe even fill in the blanks of what you can't remember. But if I ask you to write in detail about the past five minutes that is something you can do without much thought.

Great storytellers give lots of vivid details about events. With the short essay limitation you want to write lots of details about a specific event. This event or story probably takes place over a few minutes, hours, or maybe a few days. The shorter you can make the timeframe of the story, the better off you will be. You can work with an event that unfolds over days and months, but it is easier to work with a short time span. If the event spans several days or months, look for a specific event during that time that takes place over a few hours or days.

For example, your volunteer mission trip to Mexico. Instead of trying to summarize the trip, you could talk about a child you met there, Juan. You could write about how meeting him, helping him, or even how a single conversation with him changed the way you thought. That event may have taken five minutes, but you could talk about it in great detail. Make the reader "see" you, "see" Juan, and picture the detail of what happened. A specific event is much more interesting to read about and is unique to you.

Chapter 5

How to Tackle Common Questions (With Examples)

This chapter examines several of the questions asked on the Common Application and a few other common questions. Even if the college you are applying to does not use the Common Application, this chapter will be extremely useful. It will teach you how to examine essay questions, search for what is really being asked, demonstrate strategies to apply the STAR technique, offer an example answer, and analyze the key points in the answer.

Writing a great essay is a process and something that can be learned. It is no different than learning the rules and step-by-step instructions to manipulate a math problem or follow directions to build something. I am sure this notion would horrify your English teacher. It is true that use of language is an art to a certain degree, but that does not mean that there isn't a "how-to". This chapter will walk you through the step-by-step, how-to. Master storytelling, like anything else, has rules and structure. Once you understand the rules you will be able to create essays that spark interest and seem to flow. Be warned. Hard work and a little creativity are still required, but understanding the rules will keep you and your essay focused.

A few tips when forming your answers.

1) Always try to be positive. Even if the experience is negative try to look at the most positive aspects, such as what you have learned.

2) If you can, find stories where you are helping others or providing service. These type of stories come across as mature and show Admissions Officers that you will be an asset to the campus.

3) Take some time to think about your answers. Try not to use the first example that pops into your head. See if there are other possibilities or answers. Look through your lists for both Brainstorming Activities; look closely at the actions and characteristics that line up. What was the story that surrounds that? What was the problem? How did you solve it? Find the story that best answers the question prompt.

4) This is NOT easy. Give yourself a break. You are learning a new skill and that takes time and effort. If you get frustrated, take a break, and then get back to work.

5) Remember to include the details about your experiences. Before you create your answer think about the sights, sounds, and smells of the incident. It might help you to recreate it so that the reader can "see" the event through your eyes.

Some students have a background, identity, interest, or talent that is so meaningful they believe their application would be incomplete without it. If this sounds like you, then please share your story.

This question can be re-phased many ways and some version of it is most likely on your college application. Other variations might include; tell me about yourself, describe yourself, write a personal statement, or tell us about a personal experience that defines you.

Step 1: Underline the Important Parts of the Question

The very first thing you do with any essay question (College application essay, English essay, History essay, or whatever) is to read the question and underline the important parts. When I say underline, I mean it. Physically get out a pencil or pen and underline it. Most applications are online, but nothing is stopping you from printing out the prompt. Print and underline all the parts you need to answer.

Here is why. One of the most common problems students have with ANY essay is failure to answer the question asked. It makes no difference if your essay is phenomenal. If it fails to answer the question you get zero points. Sometimes you get negative points because it frustrates Admissions Officers and teachers when students don't bother to answer the question. The physical act of printing, reading, and underlining what needs to be answered will improve your ability to answer the question by 100%. After you write the essay you can look back on what you underlined to make sure you answered all the questions asked.

The important parts of this question have been underlined below.

Some students have a <u>background, identity, interest, or talent that is so meaningful</u> they believe their application would be incomplete without it. If this sounds like you, then please <u>share your story</u>.

Step 2: Determine What The Question Is Asking For

The question is asking you to share a story that defines who you are (your background, identity, interests or talents). This seems a pretty tall order. Where do you even start? So many things can define a person. You have two advantages. 1) You know they are looking for <u>a story</u>. You even underlined it. 2) You have already brainstormed your top 10 defining characteristics. Look over your defining characteristics and look at your actions from the first brainstorming activities. Any

38

seem to jump out at you? Remember you are looking for a moment in time, an event, a story that you can add detail to.

Another way to approach this step is to rephrase the question based on what you know about the person who is reading it; in this case, the Admissions Officer. What would they want to know about you after reading this essay? My translation is "Show me something interesting about yourself that I do not already know from your resume or transcript."

An Admissions Officer is reading your essay to find out something they did not already know about you. Your story needs to be about something you have not already covered in your resume. This is why small moments in time work well. Your resume may say you are President of the Honors Society, but it does not tell about the time you volunteered to teach a second grade class where you met a little girl named Mia. Mia could not keep still and refused to sit in her seat. You quickly thought of a creative way to catch her attention so you could teach the class. A story about Mia and you is interesting. A story about you finally becoming the Honors Society president is not.

Step 3: Brainstorm Story Ideas

You already have a list of your defining qualities. If you find one that seems to fit look for a story that highlights this characteristic.

A few tips on looking for the right story to express your defining characteristic. What is one of the main elements of a good story? Conflict. Conflict keeps our interest. It is what keeps us on the edge of our seat during a good movie or action flick. One of the best ways to highlight your defining characteristic is to tell a story where you overcame a problem. Look for a moment in your life where conflict exists and your defining characteristic shines through.

Remember, you are not looking for a grand event. Our lives are made of small daily events. Think about those times that might have been horrible to live through, but are funny now. Or a small moment in your life that is crystal clear. You can remember every detail about the event. Dig a little deeper into yourself and look for those small interesting moments that are unique to you.

Another tip: If you know your major, try to use a characteristic that benefits that field of study. For example, an engineer needs to have problem solving skills. Think of a time you solved a complex problem.

Hopefully you have a few ideas. If not try to brainstorming a few things you love to do. Then ask yourself what are your great character, leadership or personal qualities? Which activity exemplifies one or two of those qualities? Find your story!

Step 4: Outline And Write A Draft

Once you have a story in mind take out a piece of paper or pull up your favorite word processing program. Type or write:

S
T
A
R

Quickly look back at your underlined question. Tailor the STAR acronym to answer the question. Write down a few notes and thoughts for each letter. For this question ask yourself:

S: Situation; What's the problem?

T: Task; What do I have to do to solve my problem? Do I have any conflicting emotions concerning the task or problem?

A: Action; What specific actions did I take to solve my problem?

R: Results; What were the results and why was this event meaningful to me?

Once you have your STAR outline, start to write a rough draft. Do not worry too much about word count, grammar, or transitions. The STAR structure will help with story flow and your outline offers the bones to write about. The important part is to write something down. The first draft might not be pretty, but it is much easier to edit something than to edit a blank page. Just write it!

Example Essay (599 Words)

One hand gripped the railing and the other hand shook slightly as I reached out over the hundred foot drop toward the spotlight. My fingers and palms were slick with sweat, but I managed to twist the knob that would allow me to adjust the spotlight. I planted my feet firmly on the grated catwalk and slowly let go of the railing. It would require two hands to manipulate the spotlight and get it into position. Taking deep breaths, I forced myself to focus on the light and not look down. I moved it slightly down and to the right, so it would shine down on the stage at just the right angle. Almost there.

"Are you done yet? We still have about fifty of these to adjust. What is taking you so long?" AJ shouted from behind me. My hand slipped tightening the knob and I almost screamed. I took a quick deep breath and answered with a steady voice, "Nothing just finishing up this one. I want everything perfect for tonight." (Situation)

Along with spiders, heights haunted my nightmares. I only felt excitement a month ago when our Audio/Visual Club President asked for volunteers to help set up for the Dave Matthews Band Concert that would be held in our city's huge auditorium. Though, I might have reconsidered if I had known about the catwalks that crisscrossed the ceiling. Heights have terrified me since my brother played a stupid joke and almost pushed me off a cliff. Upon arriving that morning, I found out that our group was in charge of adjusting spotlights high above the ground. I wanted to bolt, but I promised to help. I believe strongly in honoring my commitments and decided to do my best, ignore the fear, and do what was needed. (Task)

I worked slowly and methodically adjusting spotlights that morning. I focused solely on the lights and not the hundred foot drop. As I moved across the catwalks, I looked at the wall or the next spotlight. If I felt myself begin to panic, I closed my eyes and took a deep breath. My mind chanted, "I can do this. I can do this." I felt a bit weak and breathless half the time, but I continued to do the job I was assigned. (Actions)

I envied the others who bustled past me on the catwalks, but I realized something as I tightened the last bolt. I accomplished much more than any of the other volunteers. They probably moved more spotlights, but I pushed through my fear and completed my task. It was at that moment, I realized my true potential. Society and peers try to define, put a label on, categorize, or even try to stuff people into neat boxes.

People cannot be so simply defined. I cannot be so simply defined. I can be much more than I ever imagined, if I can continue to challenge myself. I need to push past the limitations I create and not give into fear or doubt. I must continue on when others say, "You can't do that."

I look back at that moment hanging over the catwalk, terrified, and am glad I decided to honor my promise. Our crew did an excellent job and the concert went off without a hitch. I felt a deep satisfaction watching the closing act. I did not conquer my fear of heights, but I gained the knowledge that fear or doubt cannot paralyze me. I know that I have the force of will to continue to act, push past self-imposed limitations, and do what needs to be done. (Results)

In this first example, I will do more analysis than the rest of the examples. This will allow you to really get a feel of how to use the STAR technique to its fullest. (Note: I have added Situation, Task, Actions, and Results to the example essays to show you the technique. You will want to identify each part in your essay, but (and this should be obvious) don't actually type the words into your essay.)

Comments: Take note of how the story started. The reader was dropped right into the middle of the action and the "problem" became obvious quickly. Start your essay right in the mess of the situation. That will grab the attention of the Admissions Officer and they will want to read more. Give details that make the reader "see" what you saw, heard, smelled, or felt. In this example, you could see the writer's discomfort from the hundred foot drop; *hand shook slightly; fingers and palms were slick with sweat.* Picture your event in your head and relive it. What details make the scene come alive to you?

Next the writer informs you about why she is up on the catwalk and what the full scope of the task is. Even though heights are

45

one of her biggest fears, you see that following through on her commitments means more to her. The writer then details her specific actions and how she worked to cope with her fears.

Last, the essay is wrapped up with what the writer learned about herself and her abilities. She offered a broad view about what she learned, but then brought it back to the story. She told the reader that the concert went well (a result) and what she specifically learned about herself. Results and lessons are very important. Including them will make your essay standout.

Take Aways:
- Start in the middle of the action
- Use detail to make the readers see, hear, smell, or feel what you felt
- Describe your actions in detail
- Give some results from your actions (If you can offer any sort of numerical result that is even better. Example situation: Fund raising effort—raised $200)
- Offer a broad lesson learned
- End the essay by bringing your reader back to the story and what you specifically learned

The lessons we take from failure can be fundamental to later success. Recount an incident or time when you experienced failure. How did it affect you, and what did you learn from the experience?

Other variations might include; what is your greatest weakness or how do you deal with failure?

Step 1: Underline the Important Parts of the Question

The important parts of this question have been underlined below.

The lessons we take from failure can be fundamental to later success. Recount an incident or time when you experienced failure. How did it affect you, and what did you learn from the experience?

Step 2: Determine What The Question Is Asking For

On the surface, the question is asking you to share a story about a time you failed at something. What the Admissions Officer is really interested in is not the failure itself, but what you learned from it. How do you deal with/overcome failure and create a personal success from a challenge? Future performance can be predicted by past performance. If you can

47

show an Admissions Officer that your failures are a source of personal growth, then they can assume that you will continue this trend during your college years. We all fail and make mistakes. It is what we do with those experiences that shape our future. This may sound trite, but failure is an opportunity to grow and learn. Look at it this way. You could just fail and feel bad about it. Or you can look at the failure and see what you could improve upon for next time. The choice is up to you, but I prefer not to make the same mistakes over and over again.

Step 3: Brainstorm Story Ideas

Look at your action list from Brainstorming Activity #1. Look for an event where you failed. If you need to, look at the list of actions again and search for a story.

A few tips on looking for the right story. Look for an event that you can turn into a positive life learning experience. Have you tried to organize a club at school and no one showed up to the first meeting? Avoid stories about sports injuries, failing to win the game/election, or failing a class/test. Also, avoid instances in which you used poor judgment, like ditching class, crashing a car, or various acts of disobedience.

Another way to look at this question is to think about a time you said, "I'll never do that again." Not all of these moments will make good stories, but it is worth reviewing those moments for one that might work. Or think about a deep personal conviction. There is probably a story as to why you have that conviction. Something happened to you and you decided to hold to your beliefs no matter what.

For me, I believe in being honest. When I was about five, I took some candy from a store. I knew taking the candy was wrong, but I did it anyway. My dad marched me up to the manager and made me pay for it. I felt so embarrassed and scared. I felt horrible and even at that young age knew I had failed my father. After that moment, I knew that I would never steal anything again. See, there is a story behind why I feel honesty and integrity are convictions in my life. You have a story too. Look for it.

Step 4: Outline And Write A Draft

Type or write:

S

T

A

R

Look back at your underlined question. Tailor the STAR acronym to answer the question. Write down a few notes and thoughts for each letter. For this question ask yourself:

S: Situation; What's the problem?
T: Task; What was I supposed to do?
A: Action; What specific actions did I take to solve my problem? How were they effective? How were they ineffective and lead to the failure?
R: Results; What were the results, how was I affected, and what did I learn?

Once you have your STAR outline, start to write a rough draft.

Example Essay (650 Words)

My best friend Julie and I stood in the school parking lot filled with confetti and discarded food wrappers. Trash cans burst with soda cans, sticky plastic sundae cups, and partially eaten corn cobs. A few trash cans lay on their sides with flies buzzing around the spilled garbage. The place was a disaster. I looked over to the street and only saw two cars. (Situation)

"Are you sure you sent the e-mail?" Julie asked.

I sighed and answered, "I thought so."

The previous night our school held its annual Carnival Night. Our cheerleading squad was in charge of clean-up and I was in charge of getting them to do it. (Task)

Our squad had a reputation of being stuck-up and too "good" to contribute to the school. As Team Captain, I volunteered the squad to clean and hoped that would improve our reputation. Two weeks ago, I told them when and where to show up for the clean-up project and assured them it would only take an hour or two if we all helped. Most of the girls grumbled and complained. Julie supported me, but the other girls did not want to help. I reminded them that I was Team Captain and they needed to do what I said. Looking at the mess, I wondered if I should have addressed their concerns.

Julie really is a great friend. She helped me sweep the parking lot, gather the trash, and get it all to the dumpsters. It looked great when we finished, but it took six hours. I felt betrayed and absolutely furious. Not one of my other cheerleaders decided to come! Luckily, my dad talked to me before I got a chance to yell at them.

My dad saw my dismay when I returned home and sat me down to talk. After explaining the whole story, he asked me one question. Did you explain why it was important to help the school?

My anger left me. I felt sad and disappointed in myself. I realized I failed at being a leader. I told them they needed to help because I said so. I put on my Team Captain hat and told them what to do. Who was the stuck-up one now?

Monday morning came and a few of my cheerleaders asked where I was Sunday morning. Sunday? Julie and I spent Saturday cleaning up. I realized immediately what happened. First, I verbally told them about the project once, two weeks ago. Second, I sent the e-mail out late after I came back from the Carnival Night. I said "See you tomorrow." Apparently, they thought that meant Sunday due to the timing of the e-mail. I failed again. My communication skills needed work. (Action)

That moment was a turning point for me as Team Captain. I realized I needed to work harder to be a good leader and not a dictator. My attitude towards leadership and the girls changed. I began to ask them for their opinions and include them on decisions. Slowly, the whole attitude of the team changed for the better. Once I allowed other cheerleaders' ideas, they were eager to help by creating routines and taking on individual leadership roles. Eventually, a few girls offered an idea for another service project. That day, nothing could take the smile off my face.

If I ever feel the need to tell someone what to do, I think about picking up half eaten turkey legs and wrappers smeared with ketchup. I failed myself that day, but it is an experience that I will never forget. Leadership is more than a title and more than telling someone what to do. Leadership is a responsibility. A leader finds a way to get people working together. For my cheerleaders, I needed to share the spotlight and encourage their ideas. We became a team, worked together, and I found that personal improvement can come from failure. (Results)

Comments: The essay opened literally in the middle of the mess. The writer described the parking lot and the reader could "see" the mess. The problem, only two people to clean up a huge mess, became obvious fast. Also, note the use of dialogue. *"Are you sure you sent out the e-mail?"* Dialogue can break up long paragraphs and recapture the reader's interest. It doesn't always fit, but try to use a line or two in each essay. Dialogue can be an excellent tool to add interest and increase your storyteller skills.

The writer describes her task and that no other cheerleaders came to clean up. She then goes on to fill us in on the backstory and her actions that lead up to this failure of leadership. She describes her feelings and how talking to her father changed her mind. What actions she took for each of these steps was detailed and clear. She realized her own mistakes and details what she felt went wrong. When failure occurs it is important to look at what went wrong and not blame others. We cannot control others and Admissions Officers want to see self-introspection in an essay not accusations. Look at your failed actions for the essay not others. It is okay to comment on something that went wrong with others, but state it as a fact and not blame.

The writer talks about how she needed to change her ways and her feeling about the events. The results are about her turning point and what actions she took to find success from her failure. She started letting the other cheerleaders offer advice and let them take on leadership. The whole team dynamic improved due to this change. When looking for a good story for this question find something you have already worked out and implement your lessons learned. Show the Admissions Officer that not only have you learned something, but show the positive results because of it. Remember in this area of results you are looking to show results of the failure AND results from your improvements. End the essay by tying the story back to what you have learned and how your improvements have affected you or others.

Note: The first sentence in the prompt is "failure can be fundamental to later success." Try to use a story where you have already applied your lessons learned. It will provide proof to Admissions Officers that you will continue to succeed.

Take Aways:

- Start in the middle of the action
- Use detail to make the readers see, hear, smell, or feel what you felt
- Describe your actions in detail
- Give the results of the failure; do a little self-introspection here and offer how your actions lead to the failed results
- Offer your lessons learned
- Show that you have taking into account your lessons learned and implemented them
- Offer results from your lessons learned
- End the essay by bringing your reader back to the story and tying in your lessons learned with your new outlook and how it has affected you or others

Reflect on a time when you challenged a belief or idea. What prompted you to act? Would you make the same decision again?

Other variations might include; tell me about an ethical dilemma, when has your opinion been unpopular, or tell me about a time you disagreed with someone.

Step 1: Underline the Important Parts of the Question

The important parts of this question have been underlined below.

Reflect on <u>a time</u> when you <u>challenged a belief or idea</u>. What <u>prompted you to act</u>? Would you <u>make the same decision again</u>?

Step 2: Determine What The Question Is Asking For

The question is asking you to share a story about a time you challenged a belief or idea. Ethical dilemmas are excellent for this type of essay. Have you ever seen a friend/classmate cheating or stealing something? Another dilemma can be with teachers. Have you disagreed with a teacher on his classroom policies? Is there an issue at your school that students are divided by?

The trick to this question is to avoid sounding preachy or as if you are talking down to someone. The best strategy is to look for a personal event. Find a personal story in which you can express your feelings, opinions and why you felt that way. This strategy will help you come across without the negativity. Stick to the facts and your feelings, but try to tone down any negativity with what you learned about yourself.

Admissions Officers are looking to see if you are someone who stands up for what they believe in. They want to see your personal morals/ethics and how those influence your decisions. College campuses are filled with passionate students who stand up for what they believe in. Belief and passion are wonderful qualities. An Admissions Officer wants to see how you use your beliefs in a positive manner to improve the world around you.

Step 3: Brainstorm Story Ideas

Think about a time you had an ethical dilemma, disagreed with an authority figure, or had an unpopular belief. See if you can find a story in which you dealt with the situation in a positive way or learned an important lesson. Also, you can look at your list of defining qualities. A characteristic you hold dear can prompt you to act when you see something going against your beliefs.

Remember to remain positive and factual. You are not trying to lecture the Admissions Officer. You are trying to tell a story about you and engage their interest.

Step 4: Outline And Write A Draft

Type or write:

S

T

A

R

Quickly look back at your underlined question. Tailor the STAR acronym to answer the question. Write down a few notes and thoughts for each letter. For this question ask yourself:

S: Situation; What circumstances surround the issue?
T: Task; What problem or issue did I feel needed to be solved? What emotions from both sides of the issue surrounded the problem? Why did I feel the need to take action?
A: Action; What specific actions did I take to solve my problem? Did I feel conflicted about my decision?

R: Results; What were the results? What did I learn? Would I make the same decision again? Why?

Once you have your STAR outline, start to write a rough draft.

Example Essay (554 Words)

The heat soaked summer night surrounded me like a blanket constricting my breathing. I stood on the doorstep of my best friend's house and gathered my courage. My hand reached towards the doorbell and I quickly pulled it back. I wiped my palms clammy with sweat on my jeans again and tried to control my pounding heart.

"I could do this. I could do this." I chanted to myself. "How could I do this?" I moaned under my breath.

A few weeks ago, I discovered my best friend Sarah was experimenting with drugs. It seemed harmless at first. A quick drag from a cigarette laced with marijuana, but this week she had been trying serious and even dangerous drugs. She kept asking me to try them with her. I refused. She exploded and yelled that she did not want to see me again until I "loosened up." (Situation)

I was worried about Sarah. Once she started experimenting with drugs she began acting erratically and not herself. I knew she was heading towards a bad place. That is why I ended up on her doorstep that night. Sarah was out partying and I could talk to her parents. She needed help. (Task)

I reached once again for the doorbell and paused. We had been best friends for ten years. It felt wrong to go behind her back and tell her parents. I reminded myself of the rage I saw in Sarah's eyes the day before and it gave me courage. The drugs made my longtime friend a stranger. Even if she hated me for this, I knew it was the right thing to do. I loved her and did not want some substance controlling my friend. I steeled my courage and managed to quickly jab the doorbell. The door swung open and Sarah's mother smiled at me.

"Sarah's not here," she said.

"I know. Can I talk to you?" I asked.

The decision to talk to Sarah's parents filled me with conflicting emotions, but it was the right decision. (Action) Sarah's parents spoke with her that evening, and I did not see Sarah for the rest of the summer. Her parents said she was visiting an aunt. I worried about her and could not wait until school started. I entered the halls and waited by her locker. I should have expected it, but it hurt when she walked right past me. Months passed and Sarah still pretends I do not exist. My heart hurts whenever I see her. I miss my friend.

Occasionally, my mind takes me back to that night standing on the doorstep. What if I had not rang that doorbell? Would Sarah and I still be friends? Would she still be taking drugs or would she have stopped by herself? Ultimately, it does not matter. I chose to get help for a friend. Even though I miss her terribly, I made the right decision. Sarah was in trouble, and I needed to help her. I know she hates me for talking to her parents, but I still consider her my friend and want the best for her. Sometimes helping a friend is difficult. A true friend wants what is best for the other and not just what is popular or cool. A hard lesson for me to learn, but one that I would not change. (Results)

Comments: This is a hard topic and because of the question (challenging a belief) your essay might deal with a hard topic. I recommend staying away from sad topics, but notice how this topic does not focus on the "sad" portions of these events. The essay is more about the conflicting emotions the writer had and why she chose to do what she did. The essay focused on offering insights into the writer's mind and why or what she felt as she made decisions. That is the important part to this essay. You need to tell a story and then express to the

Admissions Officer why you made each decision. Then, detail what actions you took to carry the decision out.

In this essay, the writer began on a doorstep trying to decide if she should take action. You can "see" her indecision. She describes the situation and how she knows she must help her friend, but feels conflicted about how to help her. She comes to a decision and talks to Sarah's parents. What prompted her to act was the fact she knew her friend really needed help. In this essay the "actions" she took were simple. She made a decision and spoke to Sarah's parents. For this essay, it is okay for the action to be simple. The purpose of the essay centers on the internal conflict of the author.

The essay then offers the results and how Sarah will not talk to her. She expresses her sadness, but then talks about how she would make the same decision again even knowing the outcome. The author updates the reader that Sarah still hates her, but she knows she did the right thing. The essay ends with the writer offering her lesson learned; that sometimes helping a friend is difficult, but a true friend wants what is best for the other.

Take Aways:

- Make the reader feel your emotional conflict as you describe the situation; this essay is about confronting a belief or an ideal so there should be some emotional conflict
- Use detail to make the readers see, hear, smell, or feel what you felt (make sure to include what prompted you to act)
- Describe your actions in detail (sometimes the act will be simple depending on the story; use the appropriate amount of detail)
- Give the results from your actions
- Offer a broad lesson learned
- End the essay by bringing your reader back to the story and answering the question "Would you make the same decision again?"

Describe a place or environment where you are perfectly content. What do you do or experience there, and why is it meaningful to you?

Other variations might include; what do you do in your free time, what do you enjoy doing, what is your favorite activity?

Step 1: Underline the Important Parts of the Question

The important parts of this question have been underlined below.

Describe a <u>place or environment</u> where you are <u>perfectly content</u>. What <u>do you do or experience</u> there, and <u>why is it meaningful</u> to you?

Step 2: Determine What The Question Is Asking For

The question is asking you to describe a place or environment that makes you happy and why it makes you happy. The wording *place or environment* is broader than just a specific location. You can be a bit creative with this since a place or environment is really in the eye of the beholder. Do you love to run? Is your favorite place when you are in that perfect mental state where you feel like you are flying across the dirt? Do you love to babysit kids and are happiest when playing war with cardboard swords?

If I were to rephrase this question I would ask you to look for a moment or activity in your life where you were happy and felt that you were doing something great for yourself or those around you. If you can find a story about doing something for someone else and how it made you truly happy, I think that would be the best story to answer this question.

Admissions Officers are looking for students who will enhance the community and make the college campus a better place. If you can offer a story about how helping someone else made you happy, then your answer will be something special.

Step 3: Brainstorm Story Ideas

Look at your list of actions. Is there a time where helping someone made you truly happy? Or is there an activity or place where you felt like your contribution really mattered and gave you satisfaction? Is there just a place or state of mind you like to be in? Example: Running. When you reach the point in your run where to can think clearly and where nothing seems impossible. Be a little creative.

Step 4: Outline And Write A Draft

Type or write:

S

T

A

R

Quickly look back at your underlined question. Tailor the STAR acronym to answer the question. This prompt is harder to fit into the STAR acronym, but try to go through the steps to create an outline. Write down a few notes and thoughts for each letter. For this question you could ask yourself:

S: Situation; Where is that place? Describe how it feels.

T: Task; What do I feel I can accomplish, do for myself, or how can I help others?

A: Action; What specific actions did I take or could take?

R: Results; What were the results? What did I learn? Why was it meaningful to me?

Once you have your STAR outline, start to write a rough draft.

Example Essay (595 words)

Her hand gripped the pencil tight enough to make her fingers white. Kaylee thrust her other hand through her hair and yanked at it as she stared down at the almost blank piece of paper.

Suddenly, she hurled her pencil across the table and growled, "I just don't get it!" (Situation)

Two weeks ago, I undertook an impossible task. I promised a neighbor that I would tutor her daughter for an upcoming Algebra test. Kaylee needed a C on the test to pass the class. Unfortunately, Kaylee understood very little of the material and a C seemed a bit out of reach. I felt conflicted. I wanted to help, but felt powerless to really assist her. No matter which way I explained the material, she just did not understand. Then, I had a brilliant idea. (Task)

"Don't give up," I said and went to pick up the pencil. "Let's start from the beginning. What do you understand?"

The traditional methods I had been teaching Kaylee were not working. I needed to try something new. I explained my idea to Kaylee and we agreed to take a few steps back from the current material. She took me through the basic steps she did understand. We went step-by-step until she hit a roadblock. I asked her questions on what she thought should happen next and why. We struggled, but after a few minutes I grasped the concept she was missing. I created a few problems to explain the concept and then wrote out every single step required to solve them.

When finished, I handed the paper to her and asked her to look over the solutions and see if it helped. It was amazing! At first she looked puzzled, but by the second problem her face beamed with a smile. She quickly took the problem we had been working on and started to write. (Actions)

That moment when difficult concepts click and my student smiles with understanding is where I am happiest. Math concepts come easy for me, but I sympathize with those that struggle. No one is perfect and we all need help with something. I wanted to help others with Algebra and decided to become a volunteer tutor. It was the best decision I ever made. The first smile of understanding I received warmed my heart. I try to work with as many students as I can, because I love seeing a student's struggle and frustration turn to astonishment and excitement. A subject that was once such a mystery now seems clear.

Working with Kaylee and seeing her smile made me glad we persisted. We worked through a few more problems together and then it was time for her to go. She put her work in her backpack and hitched one of the straps over her shoulder. Kaylee turned back from the door and ran back to give me a quick hug.

"Thanks," she whispered.

Kaylee's thanks meant so much to me. We all struggle and have challenges in our lives. It means a lot when someone is there to lend a helping hand and it felt great to be there for Kaylee. A week later Kaylee ran to my house and banged on the front door. When I opened it, she shoved a paper in my face. In bright, red ink there was a large B. Kaylee beamed and so did I. After my experience with Kaylee, I know there is true joy in serving others. My efforts can make a positive impact and one day when I need it, others will be there to support me. (Results)

Comments: The essay opens with a frustrated student who throws her pencil. In some ways, this conflicts with the premise of the prompt, "where are you perfectly content?" Opening in the middle of conflict will draw the reader in and add interest to your essay. Especially, since the essay is supposed to be about being content. The reader finds out that the author needs to help the Kaylee improve her math grade and it has been difficult. The writer then has an idea and offers specific details on what she does to solve Kaylee's problem. This essay runs through S, T, and A before it really begins to answer the essay prompt. That's okay because the reader has been drawn into the story and now is interested in where this is going.

The author then talks about how she loves seeing that smile of understanding on a student's face. That is her place of contentment. She then gives the background on how she became a tutor and how helping others makes her happy. The end of the essay brings it back to Kaylee and the reader finds out she got a B. The writer offers her broad lesson learned, that there is joy in serving others.

This is a different approach to the question, but if you can find the right story to answer the question your essay will stand out.

Take Aways:
- Try to find a story with conflict and how your actions lead to your feeling of contentment
- Start with the conflict
- Use detail to make the readers see, hear, smell, or feel what you felt

- Describe your actions in detail
- How did the result of your actions make you feel content
- Offer a broad lesson learned
- End the essay by bringing your reader back to the story and what you specifically learned

Describe a problem you've solved or a problem you'd like to solve. It can be an intellectual challenge, a research query, an ethical dilemma-anything that is of personal importance, no matter the scale. Explain its significance to you and what steps you took or could be taken to identify a solution.

Other variations might include; tell me about a challenge in your life or what was the biggest obstacle you have overcome?

Step 1: Underline the Important Parts of the Question

The important parts of this question have been underlined below.

Describe a <u>problem you've solved</u> or a problem you'd like to solve. It can be an <u>intellectual challenge, a research query, an ethical dilemma-anything that is of personal importance</u>, no matter the scale. Explain its <u>significance to you</u> and what <u>steps you took</u> or could be taken to <u>identify a solution</u>.

Step 2: Determine What The Question Is Asking For

The question is asking you to share a story about a time you solved a problem. The question does leave it open to talk

72

about a problem you would like to solve, but it is better to share something you have done. Remember Admissions Officers are looking for students who will enhance the campus. A problem solver is always a welcome addition. Show that you take action when presented with a problem.

Step 3: Brainstorm Story Ideas

Look through your brainstorming exercises and see if an event pops up. If not look at your defining characteristics and search your mind for a problem you have solved based on your characteristics. For example, let's say you are loyal. When has being loyal helped you overcome a problem? Maybe, an untrue rumor circulated the school about your best friend. You stayed by her and supported her. Determined to help her you searched for the source of the rumor. When you found it you convinced the person to tell the truth about what really happened.

Just look for challenges in your life. Life is full of challenges so it should not be too hard to find one. Try to look for a challenge that helped you grow. A story where your actions solved a problem and you had personal growth can be a powerful essay.

Remember, the problem does not need to be life threatening or extremely personal. (Try to avoid being overly personal and making an Admissions Officer uncomfortable.) Did you resolve a dispute with a teacher, student, or boss that was difficult to deal with? Did you start a charity in honor of a lost friend or family member? Did you find a way to do the right thing when you were pressured to cheat or steal? These can be great topics.

Once you have an event in mind, begin to think about the events that led up to the problem. Think about how you initially reacted. Think about what happened as you began to gather information about the problem. What step-by-step actions did you take to solve the problem? What happened after?

Step 4: Outline And Write A Draft

Type or write:

S

T

A

R

Quickly look back at your underlined question. Tailor the STAR acronym to answer the question. Write down a few notes and thoughts for each letter. For this question ask yourself:

S: Situation; What's the problem? What events lead up to the problem?
T: Task; What do I have to do to solve my problem? How do I feel about that or the problem itself?
A: Action; What specific actions did I take to solve my problem?
R: Results; What were the results and why was this event significant to me? Did I learn something or grow from the experience?

Once you have your STAR outline, start to write a rough draft.

Example Essay (650 Words)

The rain began as a sprinkle, but then began to pour from the sky. The water level of the stream beneath my feet continued to rise. A few more minutes of rain and it would pass my knees. I held a supporting bridge beam while my friends fastened it on.

"Hurry, the stream is getting high," I yelled.

"I'm trying, but we can't find the right size bracket and bolt," Josh yelled back.

"Just use whatever you have," I called.

At the time, soaked, cold, and in a rising stream, I didn't care what bolt Josh put in. I wanted to get warm and dry. Unfortunately, that single decision became a much larger issue. (Situation)

For my Eagle Scout project, I planned to build a bridge over a stream at a local park. The community wanted to improve park safety by building a bridge. I heard about the plan and decided to make it my Eagle Scout project. I assembled volunteers, raised $1,000, and purchased the materials to build the bridge. I thought that organizing the project would be the hardest part, but I was wrong. (Task)

Josh, put the bolt in and I was able to let go of the beam. Due to the weather, we decided to come back the next day to finish up. The next day we finished up the bridge, and I sent everyone home. Only my dad remained, and we stood to admire the bridge. Dad is a contractor and wanted a close up look at the bridge. He wandered up, around, and under the bridge. Something caught his eye, and he stopped, looking at the beam that I had held up in the rain.

"What's this?" He pointed at the bracket.

I came over and explained that in the rain we could not find the correct parts. Dad frowned and explained that by law the beam needed to come down and put in with the correct parts. Due to the position of the beam, a large portion of the bridge would need to be disassembled.

"No," I said angrily. "Everyone is gone and it would take a long time to redo the work. Won't this bracket hold? The inspector approved the bridge before everyone left."

Dad felt that the bridge would still be structurally sound with what parts were in place, but it was not legal. He asked me what I wanted to do.

"As you said, the inspector did okay the bridge," he said.

I felt the weight of his stare. I did not want to spend hours fixing the bridge. The bridge was safe and would hold. Isn't that what was important? I looked into my dad's eyes and was about to tell him it was okay as is, but then I saw something on his face that made me pause. My dad always talked about other contractors who took short cuts. Some got caught and others did not, but Dad never took short cuts. He wanted to always be proud of his work and know he did it right. I wanted to feel that type of pride for my work. I wanted to know that the bridge I built was sound and would hold strong for years to come.

I made up my mind and replied, "Would you help me?" (Actions)

My dad smiled. The next day we took apart the bridge and put the correct parts in. After, we stood back and admired our work. The bridge did not look any different than the day before, but it felt different. I felt significantly different. Shortcuts or ignoring what is right might not seem like a big deal. It might not appear different to those looking from the outside, but I'll know if I take a shortcut. That day at the bridge, I committed to not taking the easy way out and to always solve my problems with what is right in mind. (Results)

Comments: I know I said to avoid generalizations of Eagle Scout projects and that is still true. This essay is an example of how to use your Eagle Scout or Mission trip experiences to create a specific story. The details of what the writer did for his Eagle Scout project is included in the story. He raised money, found volunteers, purchased materials, and built a bridge. These are important details to include, so the writer can "show-off" his Eagle Scout project, however, the project was not the focus of the essay. Instead, the story centered on the writer's moral dilemma; should he or shouldn't he spend the time to fix the bracket and bolt? Readers sympathize with this type of dilemma. We all have faced a similar situation, should we or shouldn't we take a shortcut? A story like this is interesting and shows how the writer's mind works. An Admissions Officer wants to see inside a student's head and a story like this offers a great view.

The essay begins in the rain and with the decision that causes the author problems later. The writer then walks the reader through his ethical dilemma and why he made the decision he did. He ends the essay with his determination to not take shortcuts and to do what he feels is right in the future. For this essay, it is very important to end it with what you learned. The prompt asks why this event is significant and you can easily show why it is significant if you have a life lesson.

Take Aways:
- Start in the middle of the action
- Use detail to make the readers see, hear, smell, or feel what you felt
- Describe your actions in detail (if you are using an event from an Eagle Scout project, a volunteer mission trip or any other event, make sure to detail the actions you took to

get the project to run smoothly even if it is not the focus of the story just like this example)

- Give results from your actions (This can be actual results like $1000 raised or your lessons learned or both depending on your story)
- Offer a broad lesson learned
- End the essay by bringing your reader back to the story and what you specifically learned

Discuss an accomplishment or event, formal or informal, that marked your transition from childhood to adulthood within your culture, community, or family.

Other variations might include; what moment(s) in your life changed you as a person, when did you learn or experience something that made you feel more grown-up, or what event in your life do you feel you handled maturely, like an adult?

Step 1: Underline the Important Parts of the Question

The important parts of this question have been underlined below.

Discuss an <u>accomplishment or event</u>, <u>formal or informal,</u> that marked your <u>transition from childhood to adulthood</u> within your culture, community, or family.

Step 2: Determine What The Question Is Asking For

The question is asking you to share a story about a time when you realized you weren't a child anymore. Adulthood creeps up on us and seems to surprise us one day. We spend a lot of time wishing to be older. And then almost magically, we realize we are older. At what point in time did that realization

81

occur for you? The term *event* or *accomplishment* can be loosely defined, so be a little creative.

The best essays are usually not about a big formal event like a party or awards assembly. They are usual small personal events that offer insight into the heart and mind of the student. Did your boss at your after-school job pull you aside and thank you for being trustworthy? He wanted you to know that even though his other employees were older he trusted you more and knew you would never steal from him. At that point in time, you realized your hard work and efforts were being judged like you were an adult. Another idea, could be the time you worked as a lifeguard at the pool and saved a child. You realized that being a lifeguard was more than just a job. It was a real responsibility. A responsibility you started to take more seriously, because your training helped you save a life.

Step 3: Brainstorm Story Ideas

Look over your brainstorming activity notes. Hopefully, you already have an idea for a personal story. If not another avenue to explore is your leadership experiences. Leadership is the art of getting a group of people to work together towards a common goal or objective. Leadership and its responsibility often bring out our maturity and growth toward being an adult. An example where you helped a group of people accomplish their goal and how it helped you to grow can be an excellent essay. Find two or three experiences in your life where you helped a group get to their goal. Which one of those do you feel was the most successful? What did you specifically do to make it successful?

Another thought is to look at the cultural aspect. There are many cultures where certain events are a rite of passage. This can be an excellent essay. Be careful to describe a specific moment. Avoid talking about the entire event. The more detail about why it was a turning point for you, the more interesting it will be to the reader. If you had conflicting emotions about the event, share those too (in a positive light, no complaining). Conflict will make the essay more interesting to read.

Step 4: Outline And Write A Draft

Type or write:

S
T
A
R

Quickly look back at your underlined question. Tailor the STAR acronym to answer the question. Write down a few notes and thoughts for each letter. For this question ask yourself:

S: Situation; Problem? What background is necessary?
T: Task; What did you need to do? How did you feel about it? Were there conflicting emotions?
A: Action; What specific actions did I take?
R: Results; What were the results? What new knowledge did I gain? How can I apply it to my adult life?

Once you have your STAR outline, start to write a rough draft.

Example Essay (650 Words)

One hand gripped the steering wheel. I propped the other on the top of the passenger seat as I stared through the back window. Our behemoth of a van was not the most maneuverable, and I felt nervous about backing it down the loading ramp. I turned the wheel quickly to the right so that the boat trailer would move closer to where my father waited in the boat. (Situation) Normally, I was the one waiting to guide the boat onto the trailer and Dad maneuvered it down the ramp to the water. Dad told me on our last day of fishing I would be in charge of the trailer. On previous trips, I had practiced with my Dad and uncle, but never was I allowed to

84

do this on my own. That was the moment when I knew Dad thought of me as an adult. (Task)

Our family has a male tradition to go fishing every year on Memorial Day weekend at Houghton Lake, Michigan. I loved every minute with my cousins and uncles. Three days of early morning fishing, late breakfasts at all you-can-eat buffets, and more fishing at dusk. It was a chance to relax with the males of my family and enjoy hearing about my cousins' lives and my uncles' philosophies on life. It was not until the last trip that I realized how much my life had been shaped by those yearly trips. Being one of the youngest, I gained a great deal from their conversations. I heard about my cousins' troubles with college and finding jobs just after graduation. I listened to my uncles discuss business, grumble about finances, and their love for their families. All of them had advice to offer.

I quickly glanced at my side mirrors and returned my gaze to the rear window to observe the angle of the trailer. It was not quite right. Just like my father taught me, I pulled forward and realigned the van and the trailer to get the perfect angle. I looked back to make slight twists to the wheel right or left. Small course corrections, just how I had been instructed. I yanked the wheel left a final time and got the trailer lined up just right. I backed the trailer down the ramp to the exact spot. (Actions)

"That's perfect, son," Dad called.

I had done it! Feeling great about the success, I considered what I had learned. It occurred to me that the trips to Houghton Lake and lessons on how to back up a trailer guided me towards becoming the adult I wanted to be. The talks with my cousins and their job troubles helped me decide to be very deliberate about picking my major and thinking about what I would do with my degree after college. Listening to my uncles, I discovered that family is a responsibility, but one that offers true joy. The lessons with my father and the trailer taught me not to give up on a difficult task. Sometimes you need to pull forward to fix your course completely. Other times it is best to make small course corrections to get where you want to go. Either way, you will succeed if you keep working to accomplish your goal.

The day I guided the trailer into the water highlighted the significance the annual fishing trips played in my life. In their own unique way, my family prepared me for the future. They shared advice and life lessons. They imparted hard won knowledge about family, working hard, considering what I wanted for my future, and not giving up when things are difficult. Now whenever I picture that cankerous van, I remember the pride I felt at my father's words of praise. I hold that feeling close and realize that my future is full of possibilities as long as I continue to work through challenges and make course corrections as necessary. (Results)

Comments: The story starts with the writer in the middle of backing-up a trailer. You can see he is nervous. His father entrusts this difficult task to him. He feels his father's trust is proof that his father thinks of him as a man. Now, this may not seem like a significant moment, but remember this essay is about what moment is significant to you. The most interesting and unique answers to this prompt will be about small moments like this. They are personal and connect with readers. Find your moment, no matter how small, and analyze why it is significant and what it meant to you.

The writer tells the story of backing-up the trailer and the circumstances surrounding the event. He is on an annual family fishing trip. The story weaves in what he learned from his family and how learning to handle the trailer taught him about being an adult. Then, he talks about his family's advice and how he will use it in the future. He finishes the essay by tying back into the story about making course corrections with the van and making course corrections on his life journey.

For this essay, it is very important to tie the story and your life lessons together. Make sure to weave enough of the story elements back into the life lesson, so that the reader can connect all your thoughts. Do not assume they make all the connections. Be sure to have another person read this essay and make sure to ask them what concept and ideas they got from the essay. Hopefully, their answer is the same as what you meant to say. If not go back and adjust the wording to communicate the correct ideas.

Take Aways:
- Start in the middle of the action
- Use detail to make the readers see, hear, smell, or feel what you felt
- Describe your actions in detail
- Give some results from your actions
- Offer a broad lesson learned and how this moment is significant to you and how it will help you in your adult life
- End the essay by bringing your reader back to the story and what elements of this event made you feel like an adult and how you can use that in the future

Why Are You Interested in Attending (Enter College Name Here)?

Other variations might include; how would you be a good fit for X College?

Step 1: Underline the Important Parts of the Question

The important parts of this question have been underlined below.

<u>Why</u> Are You <u>Interested in Attending</u> (Enter College Name Here)?

Step 2: Determine What The Question Is Asking For

The question is asking you why you want to go to that college. Translate this to, "What about our college specifically interests you?" Specifically, that is the key word. An Admissions Officer wants to know that you have done research and picked that college for a precise reason.

Answers such as:

My parents/friends/counselor want me to go there.

My Mom/Dad went there.

I can make a lot of money if I graduate from there.

89

This is such a great school.

I'm only here for the soccer scholarship.

You are my second choice school.

This school is close to home.

Are not exactly what an Admissions Officer would like to hear. Some or all of those reasons might be true, but you should spend a little time researching the school for other reasons. You are going to spend the next four years there. You should put a little thought into what about the college, campus, or its activities might interest you.

Step 3: Brainstorm Story Ideas

Start by getting on the school's website and doing some research. Look at your potential majors' webpages. What about each interests you academically? Look at the college's events calendar for the past year. What activities, talks, rallies, or other events interest you? If you live close, take a walking tour. See what is going on around campus. See what the atmosphere feels like and look at the various common areas where events are posted. Once you have done this come up with an academic reason you would like to go there and one or two specific extra activities you are interested in. Remember be specific!

Look at your academic reason and the extra activities you are interested in. Compare your reasons to your list of defining qualities. See what links you can find. Then, think of a story that connects your defining quality to one or two of the reasons you want to attend that college. For example, you want to attend the school because of the academic code of honor and you are very interested in the cross country team and the Helpers Service Club. A good story might be about a time during cross country practice. Your team wanted to take a short cut, basically cheat. You decided to do the whole run by yourself. You can relate that story to how you appreciate a school with an enforced honor code. You know that a school that believes in academic integrity will have a cross country team that shows integrity.

This is tricky to accomplish and you must be a bit creative in linking concepts to get it to work. It will make more sense after you read the example essay and the commentary after.

Step 4: Outline And Write A Draft

Type or write:

S

T

A

R

Quickly look back at your underlined question. Tailor the STAR acronym to answer the question. Write down a few notes and thoughts for each letter. For this question ask yourself:

S: Situation; Background?
T: Task; What do I have to do? What happened?
A: Action; What specific actions did I take to solve my problem?
R: Results; What were the results and why/how does it relate back to my desire to attend this school?

Once you have your STAR outline, start to write a rough draft.

Example Essay (623 Words)

The thick leafy branches held hints of glorious red and bright yellow, but no one was interested in the scenery. Instead, our hiking group huddled around Jill who lay on the ground. Her face was pinched with pain, and she breathed with short, harsh sounding gasps. She lay on her back with one of her legs pulled up against her chest.

Unshed tears clung to her eyes as she said, "I think my leg is broken."

That morning, our group set out to hike deep into the Sierra Nevadas. Though we followed a trail, it was a difficult climb and few ventured onto it. We made it up to the summit without incident, but on the way back Jill lost her footing and tumbled down a hill. We hurried down to her and knew from the look on her face it was bad. (Situation)

Her words spurred me into action. Years of first aid classes came to my mind and I knew what to do. (Task) I told the group to find me two long thick sticks and to give me a few of their bandannas. I broke the sticks to the proper length and tied them to her leg using the bandannas. I surveyed my handy work. Not too bad, but we still had the problem of getting her down the mountain trail. I told two people from our group to head down the hill and get help.

It was mid-afternoon, and I knew that it would be impossible for help to get to us before dark. The next few miles were the steepest and if we could get her down those it would be easier for the rescuers. I looked at Jill. She still looked shaken, but most of the intense pain had left her face.

"Jill, if we helped support your weight and kept it off your leg, do you think you could make it a few miles?" I asked.

"I think so," Jill replied.

My life's goal is to become a doctor. I have taken many first aid classes and I am CPR certified, but this was the first time my training had been tested. The cuts and scrapes I doctored for my younger sisters were nothing compared to a broken leg in the middle of nowhere. Regardless, when I saw Jill hurt I felt competent enough to help. Our group took turns supporting both of Jill's sides and helping her down the hill. (Actions) About two miles from the trailhead, we saw our rescuers. They arraigned Jill on a stretcher and carried her the rest of the way. I sat on a rock watching them and the intensity of the moment sunk in. I acted calm under the pressure. My actions made sure Jill was a little more comfortable and got her to help faster.

Jill's accident validated my desire to become a doctor. I liked feeling knowledgeable enough to help her. That's why I want to attend College X. College X has an excellent reputation for preparing undergraduates for medical school. I am especially interested in meeting and working with Professor Smith. His research on opportunistic infections in immunocompromised transplant patients fascinates me. Also, I am excited to join the Hiking Club on campus. The annual two-day trek through

Smoky Mountains sounds challenging and fun. I might even try an excursion or two with the Spelunking Club.

College X would help me fulfill my dream of becoming a doctor. The combination of the staff, the research they are doing, and the excellent reputation of the school can attest to that. Besides academics, the school has outdoor activities that interest me. After caring for Jill and getting her down the mountain, I am prepared for the challenge College X will bring. (Results)

Comments: This essay begins with a fall scene and a girl lying hurt in the woods. The problem is obvious and the reader is interested in how it happened and what the author will do. The reader finds out that writer had first aid training. She then goes on to describe exactly what she does to help Jill and talks about her plan to get her help. The writer appears confident and capable. The reader discovers her training is due to her desire to become a doctor.

The final part of the essay ties in her desire to be a doctor, her interest in hiking, AND her specific reasons for wanting to attend the school. This seems a tall order, but if you do the research on why you specifically want to go to a school this will become easier. In this essay, the writer wants to be a doctor, the school has a good medical program and she knows that a Professor is researching an area she is interested in. She uses her story about hiking to show her interest in hiking and her interest in the school's Hiking Club. She finishes with mentioning Jill and how after helping her she knows she is read for the challenge of the college.

Do the research, find out why you want to go to a school. Find both academic and extra-curricular reasons. Look for a story in your extra-curricular activities that can tie everything together.

Take Aways:
- Start your story in the middle of the action
- Use detail to make the readers see, hear, smell, or feel what you felt
- Describe your actions in detail
- Talk about the results and how this ties back to your interest in the school
- Offer school specific academic interests and extra-curricular ones
- Bring the reader back to the story and wrap everything together to create a coherent essay

Who has influenced you the most over your lifetime?

There are several versions of this question. Who is your hero? What is your favorite fictional character? Who do you admire most? Who do you admire most in history?

Step 1: Underline the Important Parts of the Question

The important parts of this question have been underlined below.

<u>Who</u> has <u>influenced you the most</u> over your lifetime?

Step 2: Determine What The Question Is Asking For

The question is asking who has shaped you and your actions. The question does not directly ask for a story, but stories make the best and most interesting answers. So find a story!

The interviewer is not necessarily interested in who, instead they are more interested in why you admire them or what type of influence they have had over your life. You need to articulate the qualities or characteristics that you admire and how that has influenced you.

Step 3: Brainstorm Story Ideas

Start by identifying three or four qualities you admire most. Depending on the prompt, what real person, fictional character, and historic individual exemplify one or two of those qualities?

Think about a time where that person displayed those qualities. Conflict often highlights great qualities. Always look for stories with conflict (a problem to solve). Share the story. Make sure to talk about why you admire those qualities and how they have affected your life. Be aware that a relative is one of the most common answers to this question. Many might caution you to NOT use a relative. Personally, I think using a relative is fine, but you MUST tell a story. Catch the attention of the Admissions Officer with the story. If you tell a good story it doesn't matter who you admire most.

You must focus on what qualities you admire then pick a story about that person that highlights those qualities. Most students who pick a relative just say they admire the person and then offer reasons why. You can be different by "showing" why you admire that person through the story. Family is often one of the most central parts of young students' lives and it is to be expected that they have the most influence. Don't be afraid to use family, but focus on the details of the story and how you feel or were affected during those events. Remember to look for a story with conflict. We are all fascinated with problems and conflict.

Step 4: Outline And Write A Draft

Type or write:

S

T

A

R

Quickly look back at your underlined question. Tailor the STAR acronym to answer the question. Write down a few notes and thoughts for each letter. For this question ask yourself:

S: Situation; What's the problem?
T: Task; What did that person need to do?
A: Action; What specific actions did he/she take to solve the problem?
R: Results; What were the results? Why do I admire those qualities and how has it influenced my life?

Once you have your STAR online, start to write a rough draft.

Example Essay (644 Words)

Why exactly I stood dressed in tattered clothes, covered in fake blood, and surrounded by a group of undead still remains a mystery to me. My only explanation centers on the fact that my Aunt Kristie is the most amazing person I know. Due to her influence, I was up at five in the morning and by six my face had been covered in itchy, peeling face putty. I looked and felt the part of a zombie. The crisp fall air did nothing to wake my senses or calm my feelings of unease. I hated zombie anything. The whole idea of the walking undead gives me the creeps, but there I stood as one of them waiting for the gun to go off. (Situation)

The trouble began a few days ago when the flu hit our area hard. Everyone seemed to be sick and unfortunately for me, most of my Aunt's volunteer zombies were down with the flu. Did that stop Aunt Kristie form helping a family who lost their house in a fire? No, of course not. Aunt Kristie was determined to make her Zombie Run a success. She is the most strong-minded person I know and always comes up with plans to help others.

She is an avid runner and thought that a Zombie run would be a fun way to raise money for a family who lost everything in a fire. She planned the event and thanks to her social media skills she sold out of runner slots. Runners were coming in from all over the country to help out and have a good time. Each hoped to make it through the obstacles and hordes of zombies intact, without losing all of their health flags. As a zombie it was my job to try to grab a runner's health flag. It was all in the name of fun, but I wished the flu had avoided our town. (Task)

When Kristie heard that everyone was sick, she immediately called in favors from out of town friends and everyone in my family who was out of bed. Secretly, I think my grandmother was excited to dress up and chase after people. Not me. I explained to my Aunt why I could not do it. Zombies made my skin crawl and a bit sick to my stomach. Did I mention that my aunt is amazing? A few words from her describing the family's loss, and I was nodding yes.

Bang! The sound of the starting gun brought me back to my purpose, and I readied myself to shamble after the first group of runners on this charity Zombie Run. I spent the day lunging at yellow flags and jumping from behind trees to scare runners. By the end of the day, I decided that the event had been fun and I even enjoyed myself a bit. (Actions)

It is events like the Zombie Run and her ability to coerce even me into helping, why I admire my Aunt. She is a whirlwind of life and always ready to help others. She see a problem and tackles it head on. She creates lists, plans, and organizes others into effective teams. Throughout my life she has always been there for me and helped me step through my problems one little step at a time. From her example, I have learned the value of taking a problem apart and finding ways to solve it. Her enthusiasm to help others is so contagious and even if you are reluctant she has a way of convincing you to help out. I am still not a fan of zombies, but I feel proud to have been a part of a charity event that raised over $10,000 for a family in need. Due to Aunt Kristie's influence, my problem solving skills are sharp and her example fills me with a desire to help others. (Results)

Comments: The essay begins with the author in an unlikely place, dressed as and surrounded by the undead. Furthermore, he does not want to be there. The reader finds out his aunt Kristie has talked him into helping out. He acknowledges that it is only due to her persuasive personality he is there. The story gives us Kristie's task, to put on a Zombie run for charity, and details her actions when her original plan does not work. Throughout the story, the reader can see the admiration the author has for his aunt. In this essay, the story is about Kristie, so details are centered on her and her specific actions. Through the zombie event, the reader gets a sense of why Aunt Kristie is such a big influence on his life.

The essay then brings the reader back to the race with a "bang" of the starting gun. He talks about how he actually had fun and specifically points out what about his aunt has influenced him. Because of the story the reader can really "see" why he admires her. He was proud to be a part of such a successful charity event (note how the $10,000 number was stated---if possible include a number as part of the results). He closes the essay with his lesson learned and ties the details of the story into the lesson.

This essay is an excellent example of why a story is the way to catch an Admissions Officer's attention. Imagine reading a thousand or more essays on why someone has influenced a student. I promise you they will ALL blend together, because they are all nice and very predictable reasons. After about a thousand warm and fuzzy reasons why a student admires someone they all sound the same. Now, a story about a Zombie Race? That is something interesting to read about. The essay is focused on the story, but through the author's narration of the story the Admissions Officer "sees" why Aunt Kristie is so admired. A story with specific reasons and examples is much more interesting to read about.

Take Aways:

- Start in the middle of the action
- Use detail to make the readers see, hear, smell, or feel what you felt as you watched the person you admire go through the "story"
- Describe the actions of the person you admire in detail; show the reader why you admire them
- Give the results
- Detail what about the person's action and even the results from the story you admire; how has that influenced you?
- End the essay by bringing your reader back to the story and what you will take from that and apply to your life

Chapter 6

Write it, Leave it, Edit it

Write it

Remember once you finish the outline start writing! Do not worry about word count, perfect grammar, or trying to make it extraordinary the first time through. The first version is a draft! It is okay if the essay falls short of your expectations. The important part is to get your thoughts on paper. Once you have something, edit it and make revisions. By the end of the process, it will be extraordinary. Take a quick read-through after and do some basic editing. You can fix spelling and obvious grammar mistakes, but do not worry about too much else. Now, leave it and do something else.

Leave it

This concept might seem counter-intuitive. I just told you to write all your thoughts down, now I want you to let it sit? Yes. It can be difficult to edit your own work. You wrote it. You can easily fill-in any assumptions, details left-out, or leaps in logic. The essay might make perfect sense to you, but the reader might feel a bit lost or make an incorrect assumption. You are trying to communicate to an Admissions Officer and you need to look at your essay as a stranger would.

That is why it is best not to do a detailed edit immediately. It works best if you can let it sit for a day or two. Hopefully, you have started your essays early so you have some time. You can always work on the next essay. Let's say you have five essays to write. Write the draft of the first. Then, work on the draft of the second. Continue until you have drafted all five essays. Next, go back and start editing the first. Basically, work your way through the essays in a set order and then start at the beginning when done.

I recommend making a schedule for yourself. As an example, you have five essays, and you make a plan to draft one essay per day. That means five days to write the five drafts. Then, you can edit two essays per day. That will be another two to three days. You are going to want to do a second edit, so plan another two to three days for a second edit. Creating an extraordinary essay takes time and effort to work your way through the process. That is why it is important to start early and create a schedule that makes sense for you. Do not plan on writing five extraordinary essays in a week before they are due. It is possible, but improbable. Your essay quality will suffer.

Edit it

I talked a bit about a leave it and edit it schedule above. You need to plan in time to do a second edit. Also, you need to plan time in for friend(s) or parent(s) to read through and offer advice. If you are on a tighter schedule, you could give your friends/parents each a set of first-time edited essays as you complete them. Hopefully, you will get each set back in time to start your second edit cycle. Remember the key is to start early.

Tips for Editing

- **Write your essays in a word processing program**: Many colleges have online forms that you must submit your essays through. DO NOT write your essay in the online field. Write it in a word processing program and copy and paste it in. As an Admission's Officer, I read so many essays that were obviously written in the online field. They were riddled with spelling and grammar errors and barely edited.

- **Spell Check & Grammar Check**: You would be surprised at how many essays I read that were not spell checked. The grammar check works okay, but it does not replace a manual grammar check. You need to read through and check it. The grammar check misses words in context. The grammar might be correct, but you could have typed the wrong word.

- **Now you edit it**: Do a first pass edit and find the obvious errors. Look for grammar, flow, and if you feel you have set-up and made your point. Be sure to look at the prompt and make sure you've addressed all the questions.

- **Look for**: Various sentence length; Specific descriptions; Use a thesaurus for synonyms, so you do not continuously use the same word. Just make sure to use words you would normally use and not big SAT/ACT words just for show. Don't go overboard on adjective and adverb usage.

- **Read it out loud**: Print your essay and read it out loud. It is important to print the essay and not read it off a computer screen. Your eyes and mind will see new things once you vary where you are reading from. Also, reading out loud will help you listen for sentence flow and "hear" errors you may not see by reading it in your head.

- **Read it by starting at the last sentence**: Another self-editing method is to read your essay one sentence at a time beginning at the last sentence. Read the last sentence, then read the second to last sentence, and so on until you finish. Reading it backwards will help you get a bit of distance from the writing and help you spot grammar and other errors.

- **Have at least two others read it**: Remember you are trying to communicate to someone who does not know you well. It is important to have another brain or two reading your essay. They will see things that you do not and they can tell you if you are effectively getting your point across. Have them read it and then ask them what are the main points or ideas they got from the essay. If they differ from what you were trying to convey, ask where they got those ideas. You can reword your sentences to better communicate your ideas or true meaning.

- **Leave it and go back in a few days to edit it again**: Take a break for a few days on that particular essay. A bit of time away from it will help you see errors you missed before. Edit another essay while you let that one sit. When a couple of days have passed got back and do the second self-edit.

- **Font and Font Size**: If you are printing and sending in your essays (rather than an online form) use a common font like Times New Roman or Arial or other easy to read font. Do not be creative, just make it easy for the Admissions Officer to read. Also stick to an 11 or 12 size font. Follow any directions about spacing; single, double, or whatever is specified.

- **Word Count**: This is important. You MUST adhere to the word count. If there is a minimum or a maximum stick to those numbers. It annoys Admissions Officers when students don't follow directions. You do not want the person reading your file to be annoyed or upset with you. Get credit for your work, not criticism because you could not be bothered to follow directions.

Always do a quick word count and spell check one last time before hitting send! You might have had a few last minute corrections. It is important and will provide peace of mind if you do one last check!

Chapter 7

Checklists

This chapter contains a few checklists that you can run through once you have completed your essay. Depending on the question, some of the items below may not apply.

Situation

- Did you start in the "heat" or middle of the action?
- Details, details. Did you use details to make the readers see, hear, smell, or feel what you felt?

Task

- Does the reader have enough information/backstory to make the context of the problem and task make sense?
- Does the reader have a sense of where the story/essay is heading at this point?
- Have you expressed to the reader your feelings about the problem/task? (Conflicting emotions are okay and very human.)
- Can the reader feel your emotions/pain? Can they sympathize with you?

Actions

- Did you detail the specific actions you took?

- How do/did you feel about your actions?

Results

- Did you give results from your actions (If you can offer any sort of numerical result that is even better. Example situation: Fund raising effort—raised $200)
- Did you offer a broad lesson learned?
    - Did this event change the way you thought or will act in the future?
    - Did you learn something about yourself, others, or the world?
- Did you end the essay reminding your reader about the story and how it affects you today or what you learned and are going to do in the future?

In General

- Does the essay reflect that you are competent and self-confident?
- Do you appear humble and likeable? (You can be self-confident and humble at the same time. Have someone read it and ask if you appear likeable. If you focus on the story and the positive aspects of what your learned this should be an easy one.)

Did you avoid?

- Any kind of list

- Slang

- Trendy or Pop Culture References

- Sad topics like divorce, death, or loss

- "The most important thing"

- Sports

- "I am so thankful for"

- Comparisons

- Broad volunteer activities to include

  - Eagle Scouts
  - Mission trips
  - Camps

- Trips to visit the campus

- Any event the college sponsored

- Rude or unprofessionally expressed opinions

- Sensitive topics

- Illegal activities

Final Thoughts Before Submitting

- Does my essay answer all the question(s) in the prompt?
- Did I follow all of the formatting or other directions given by the application?
- Did I do a final spell/grammar check?
- Did I do a final word count?

Writing an extraordinary essay takes some time and is not easy, but it is something you can learn to do. If you use the STAR method and follow the tips in this book, you CAN write an extraordinary essay. With each essay you write you will find that it gets easier and ideas start to flow. The real trick is to start early so you have time to have others help you edit. Also, if you get stuck you can take a break and start again the next day.

Now that you have the right tools and a solid process, you CAN do this! It's time to get started. Work through the brainstorming activities, outline your STAR stories, and then write that all important first rough draft. After your first draft, the rest of your essays will seem much easier.

Getting started is really the hardest part. Don't waste another minute. Pick up a pen and get started. You CAN do this. I believe in you.

Thank you for reading this I enjoy demystifying the college essay for students. If you found it helpful please consider reviewing it on Amazon. Reviews help other students find this great resource for writing college essays.

If you enjoyed this book and need additional help consider picking up one of my other books.

Check out my website at www.CollegeEssayNinja.com

Extraordinary College Essay Workbook: The Ultimate Guide to Brainstorming your College Essay: Need additional help brainstorming you college essays? This workbook walks you through the brainstorming exercises with space to write and make notes as you work.

I Can Ace My College Interview: Perfect if you need to accomplish an interview for college or for a scholarship.

Made in the USA
Lexington, KY
27 October 2015